LIZ LOCHHEAD

Liz Lochhead is a poet, playwright and occasional theatre director. She was born in Lanarkshire in 1947 and educated at Glasgow School of Art. Her collections of poetry include *Dreaming Frankenstein*, *The Colour of Black & White* and *True Confessions*, a collection of monologues and theatre lyrics.

Her original stage plays include *Mary Queen of Scots Got Her Head Chopped Off*, *Blood and Ice*, *Perfect Days* and its 'sister play' *Good Things*. Her many stage adaptations include *Dracula*, Molière's *Tartuffe*, *Miseryguts* (based on *Le Misanthrope*) and *Educating Agnes* (based on *L'École des Femmes*); as well as versions of *Medea* by Euripides (for which she won the Scottish Book of the Year Award in 2001), and *Thebans* (adapted mainly from Sophocles' *Oedipus* and *Antigone*).

Liz lives in Glasgow. She became the city's Poet Laureate in 2005.

Liz Lochhead

BLOOD AND ICE

NICK HERN BOOKS
London
www.nickhernbooks.co.uk

A Nick Hern Book

This revised version of *Blood and Ice* first published in 2009 by Nick Hern Books Limited, 14 Larden Road, London W3 7ST

Published in an earlier version in 1985 in *Plays by Women: Vol. 4* (Methuen Drama)

Cover image: *The Nightmare* (1781) by Henry Fuseli (The Detroit Institute of Arts / The Bridgeman Art Library)
Cover design: Ned Hoste, 2H

Typeset by Nick Hern Books, London
Printed in the UK by CPI Antony Rowe, Chippenham, Wiltshire

A CIP catalogue record for this book is available from the British Library

ISBN 978 1 84842 061 8

Introduction

Blood and Ice, my first play, was performed in its first full incarnation at the Edinburgh Festival Fringe in August 1982 at the Traverse Theatre in Edinburgh with Gerda Stevenson perfectly cast as Mary. She was lovely. Young, heartbreakingly young was how she played it, in love with a poet and with a poetic ideal, earnest, passionately enquiring, passionately committed to living a life that secretly terrified her.

Nevertheless, the play, even by its kindest critics – and, yes, there were some of those – could not possibly be called an unqualified success. It was far too long for one thing, and was, literally, all over the place. I, for one, must admit that I can't, now, make head or tail of the original script, although within its excesses I can see it also contains what proved to be the still-beating heart of the whole creature, which is an exploration of the sources, and the consequences for its creator, of an enduring and immortal myth.

Mary Godwin Shelley lived at the cusp of reason and romanticism. She was the daughter of two great Age of Reason radical philosophers of freedom: William Godwin, author of *Political Justice*, and Mary Wollstonecraft, author of *A Vindication of the Rights of Woman,* a founding feminist who died of puerperal fever just one week after giving birth to Mary. This legacy weighed heavily upon the child. As did, later, her own female biological destiny.

So much for free love. From the age of sixteen, when she ran away with him, married already as he was, until the death of Shelley eight years later when she was only twenty-four, she herself was almost constantly either pregnant, recovering from miscarriage or mourning the death of a child. (Only one, the delicate Percy Florence, was to survive into adulthood.) So many deaths. The suicides of her own Shelley-obsessed sister and Shelley's deserted wife were sore enough but, far worse, the deaths of so many little innocents – their own, and the child of her stepsister and Byron too, all dragged around Europe in that ultimate romantic pursuit of their progenitors. No surprise perhaps that, prescient as she must have been – many, though not all, of these griefs lay ahead of her – this particular seventeen-year-old girl should have come up with a deep-felt fantasy of *a new way of creating life*. She was already, I'm sure, subconsciously aware of pushing herself beyond her own natural boundaries. Therefore the myth emerged as far from Utopian, but one of horror and terror of Science, a myth that remains potent for our nuclear age, our age of astonishment and unease at the fruits of perhaps-beyond-the-boundaries genetic experimentation.

That garbled first script of mine nevertheless contains, more or less verbatim, many of the scenes which are still extant in this version, the umpteenth and, I have promised myself, final version, which was completed for a 2003 production in the Royal Lyceum Theatre in Edinburgh instigated by, and directed by, Graham McLaren, with whom in the last decade I have collaborated on several versions of classic plays for Theatre Babel.

Many young directors, many young actors, university students and struggling new fringe companies have, since 1982, taken on the challenge of this play. I have met quite a few since who were keen to tell me: 'This was the first play I found for myself and just knew I had to direct it'; or 'I played Byron'; or 'I was Shelley'; or 'I loved playing Mary.' Many of these productions, the ones I saw at any rate, had wonderful *moments*. They'd fire me up and get it going again for me. I got on with trying to write other plays, but, all through the 1980s, like a dog returning to its own vomit, I'd go back to it, trying, abortively, to solve the problem of the structure, find what would finally seem the satisfactory form, keeping up the pursuit myself – for its own sake, whether there was an upcoming production or not – happily scribbling away through long lonely nights, just as obsessively, I had to own, as half-mad Frankenstein himself labouring with his unlovely creation, looking for the spark of life.

That spark came towards the end of the decade when, in 1988, David McVicar, now world-famous as a director of opera, but then a second-year student at Glasgow's Royal Scottish Academy of Music and Drama, phoned me up and said he

wanted to direct the play and had a cast together for a
production at the Edinburgh Festival Fringe.

I remember saying, 'Don't do it. Yes, it has great ideas in it,
and a couple of great scenes, but it doesn't actually *work*.'

David said, 'I know, but I think I can see what's wrong with
it. Can we have a coffee and talk?'

I met David. Then went to a rehearsal and fell in love with
the cast. It had to be a real ensemble piece and they were a real
ensemble. So young, so talented and full of fire. I felt: hey, this
lot might actually be about to crack it...

They got me doing, for nothing of course, but happily,
obsessively again, loads and loads of work, more midnight oil,
on a new script, one very, very like this one published here.

David McVicar's production in its Edinburgh Fringe Scout
Hall venue was thrilling. It was alive! Candlelit, and in 1960's
cheesecloth shirts and loon pants and simple long hippy-chick
dresses for the girls, it had an amazing *coup de théâtre* when,
from under the alpine peaks of an unmoving heap of muslin, the
Creature, at the end of the first act, naked and beautiful as a
baby, suddenly stood up and made the audience gasp — and
terrified Mary into sitting down to write.

The cast were fantastic. Wendy Seager's Mary, Daniela
Nardini's Claire (for the first time not *merely* an annoying idiot
of a millstone for Mary but also passionate, and pitiable, a
convincingly whole, if not well-rounded, person asserting,
painfully, her own right to love), John Kazek's brooding Byron
and John Straiton's incandescent Shelley were all so young and
so beautiful they had charm enough to make us actually care
about this set of self-indulgent, if brilliant, adventurers.

They were invited to perform their production at the
Traverse that autumn, and RSAMD gave them leave of absence
from the final year of their course to do so. It was sold out and
there were queues for returns. When they had graduated, *Blood
and Ice* was the first production of David McVicar's far too
short-lived touring company Pen Name.

A ghost, for me, was laid to rest.

When, half a dozen years ago, Graham McLaren came to me
wanting to do *Blood and Ice* on the big stage of Edinburgh's
Royal Lyceum, I said, '...yes – but, oh, it's practically
impossible to bring off, the actors must be really, really young,

and also credibly these brilliant poets, and be gorgeous, and charming, especially Shelley, whom I haven't ever managed to make so enough in the script, and they must all be human and vulnerable, even Byron – and you'll have to make sure they find a lot of laughter and lightness in the opening scene, and some playful, joyful and easy sensuality too, because there is so little of that shown as the play begins at the point the cracks are appearing, and because there is so much darkness ahead in the journey. And, Graham, for the big stage, I'll really have to have a wee go at the *structure*…'

Graham's production, with another lovely young cast, was very beautiful, very spooky, very romantic and made me very happy.

It's exactly thirty years since I first took down from a library shelf Muriel Spark's *Child of Light*, her wonderful biography of Mary Shelley, and, shortly after, began my own pursuit. Could I make a play…? Naively, I was, at the time, quite blithely unaware that I wasn't the first, and certainly wouldn't be the last, to be fired by the dramatic possibilities of this moment in history, that iconic stormy summer of 1816 by the shores of the lake and beneath the high Alps. There is, apparently, a 1969 novel called *A Single Summer with L.B.* by Derek Marlowe, which since someone told me about it twenty-odd years ago, I've always meant to read. And now that I really am finally through with these characters for myself, I will. There was a fairly terrible Ken Russell film called *Gothic* in 1986; and also Howard Brenton's 1989 stage play *Bloody Poetry,* which focused on Shelley's radical romantic politics – and Byron. But, as for *Blood and Ice,* this published version is the very last word from me on these characters, this particular dilemma.

Unless, David McV, you know someone you can persuade this old play of mine could be a brilliant, blazing brand-new opera…?

Liz Lochhead
July 2009

This version of *Blood and Ice* was first performed at the Royal Lyceum Theatre, Edinburgh, on 24 October 2003, with the following cast:

MARY SHELLEY	Lucianne McEvoy
SHELLEY	Phil Matthews
BYRON	Alex Hassel
CLAIRE CLAIRMONT	Susan Coyle
ELISE	Michele Rodley

Director   Graham McLaren

Characters

MARY SHELLEY
PERCY BYSSHE SHELLEY
CLAIRE CLAIRMONT
LORD BYRON
ELISE, *a maid*
THE CREATURE
NURSE

ACT ONE

In an England of darkness and loneliness, MARY SHELLEY, *a young widow in her late twenties, is stretched out asleep.*

The 'nightmare is upon her', the image is that of the famous Fuseli painting and there is perhaps an actual and physical manifestation of the smothering homunculous on her chest that appears momentarily in a flash of lightning and disappears again in the beat of darkness that follows it. Certainly, shadows move. A dream whisper breaks her sleep.

CREATURE'S VOICE. Why did you make me?… Frankenstein?

MARY *wakes with a gasp of fear. Dead silence. She breathes, listening. Wind blows the window open, it bangs once, twice, three times. She gets up and, barefoot, pads across the floorboards to fasten it, her relief palpable.*

Ideal or important pieces of set and furniture are a double-sided oval mirror on a stand (a cheval glass) and a night-marish perhaps oversized rocking horse. It rocks now of its own will, but when MARY *turns around, it stops.*

MARY (*sighing relief*). Nothing.

CREATURE'S VOICE (*a whisper*). Frankenstein?

MARY. Such dreams.

Night after night, such bad dreams.

I go to my new book, for I will write it, I must!

And dreams of that old one, the one that's done and dusted, in print and out there in the world, making whatever stumbling way it can, for better or worse – dreams of my infamous creation come back to haunt me.

Come back to haunt me and I cannot shake it off.

I have the strongest presentiment something terrible is about to happen.

Last night I dreamed, I dreamed I was seventeen, we were back in Poland Street, I found my little baby, my firstborn, it was not dead but... cold merely. Shelley and I rubbed it before the fire and it lived! Awoke and found no baby.

No Shelley.

CREATURE'S VOICE. Why?

MARY. Don't think of him.

When they found him washed up, his eyes, his face, all parts of him... not protected by his clothes were eaten away, they only knew him by – in his pocket they found... that volume of Keats he carried with him always.

Sometimes I wake up. Cold. Bathed in a moon sweat. And I rub myself slowly to life again.

The dead of night.

Don't think of him.

More movement, shadows, and suddenly:

SHELLEY'S VOICE. Oh, Mary! You don't seem to care how much it grieves me that you won't sail with me...

Come and see her.

New arrived from Genoa, *The Ariel*, the bonniest boat that ever sailed the seas!

MARY. Don't think of him.

She goes to her writing desk with great effort of will.

Loud cries of 'Mama, Mama, Mama' and suddenly a very flesh and blood bonny wee six-year-old CHILD *with girlish soft long fair hair, runs in, capering with a toy windmill or a ball, some toy in motion.* MARY, *laughing, runs and catches him up and tickles him. He giggles and squirms.*

Oh, Perciflo, you rascal! Your mama's best boy, her only! What am I to do with you! Your mama is busy, she must write her new storybook and earn lots of pennies for her big bonny best boy!

Nurse! Nurse! Come and fetch him, please!

NURSE *appears, a quick in-and-out shadow of a girl who takes the* CHILD, *kicking, under her arms, and exits with him.* MARY *calls offstage after them.*

See Percy Florence gets to bed again and has himself a proper night's sleep – and no argument about it, my naughty little, my nice little, my naughty little man!

Alone again, she sits at her work.

My sweet, sweet boy, my only consolation…

Oh, how am I to take care of you, all by myself?

This new book of mine will save us both. Must! *The Last Man*… such a good fantastical idea for a philosophical and terrifying novel. If I work constantly on this one and manage a mere thousand words a day, then in only a hundred days… allow two more months for copying and revisions and… surely on the strength alone of the stir that surrounded my last publication –

CREATURE'S VOICE. Frankenstein, why did you make me?

MARY. Well, it wasn't for the money anyway. Nor for the wager, or the challenge of the competition –

Shadows move.

BYRON'S VOICE. I'll set us a little contest. Why should we content ourselves with translated, traditional horrors, all bookish and stilted. Home-grown ones are the best. Who can make the most stirring unnatural tale?

MARY. There were three of us.

SHELLEY'S VOICE. Mary!

BYRON'S VOICE. Mary!

CLAIRE'S VOICE (*a giggle*). Mary!

MARY (*as if silencing her*). There were *three* of us!

Shadows move.

ELISES'S VOICE. Mrs Shelley, madame! Milord Byron's man says he is here to fetch both the ladies –

MARY *firmly suppresses these voices from the past.*

MARY. There was Shelley... and Byron... and me.

CREATURE'S VOICE *overlaps and echoes.*

CREATURE'S VOICE. Me... Me... Me!... Tell me about the night you made me, Frankenstein.

MARY *blows out the candle, casts off her heavy, dark dressing gown and is a laughing eighteen-year-old in white muslin back in Switzerland, 1816 – summer, daytime, in a totally bright and different light. The lake and Mont Blanc above it.*

Wet and naked, capering, SHELLEY, *a boy of twenty-two, wrapped only in a lace tablecloth, spins her round and kisses her.*

SHELLEY. Mary Godwin, you are such a prude! Such blushes! Come here until I kiss them better.

MARY. Shelley, how could you? Honestly... put some clothes on.

SHELLEY. Swimming, Mary. I want to learn to swim.

MARY. Walking naked across the terrace, all tangled up with weeds and –

SHELLEY. I forgot. I forgot they were coming.

MARY. You did not! You only wanted to be outrageous –

SHELLEY. Oh, what does it matter, Mary!

MARY. It matters to me! She was a great friend of my mother's.

SHELLEY. Old humbugs, pretending to be shocked!

MARY (*fighting laughter*). I thought La Gisborne would have an apoplexy!

SHELLEY. And the other old goose! Lord, I thought she was going to burst her goitre.

MARY (*laughing*). Thank goodness they've gone! They didn't stay a minute after your grand apparition, though! It was make excuses and off before they'd drained their first teacup. Oh, Shelley, how could you have! Naked!

SHELLEY. I covered myself! Just as soon as I saw you had company to tea. I had two choices. I could brazen it out, or hide myself behind the maidservant. So I –

MARY. What Elise must have thought I cannot imagine!

SHELLEY. Oh, so not content with fretting over the old dowagers, now we are to agonise over the imagined offence to the servant girl! Well, at least we don't have to worry about what the neighbours will say.

MARY. It's his influence makes you so careless of the regard of others!

SHELLEY. No, Mary, you know I never cared for the world's approval. Not in such… silly and private matters. And neither did you! The Mary I met…

MARY. Did not go deliberately out of her way to offend elderly ladies in such… silly and trivial ways!

SHELLEY. I covered myself. Dodging behind the maidservant, swaddling myself in her apron strings. I twirled around and, sleight of hand, snatched out the topmost tablecloth like a conjurer ere she put down the tea things and sat myself down, decently draped in dimity and lace, to adequate small talk amid the tinkling cups. I do not see how you can begin to complain of me!

MARY. I was surprised enough when they called in the first place. You know how our position makes us vulnerable to... of course, Maria Gisborne was a follower of Mama's, certainly she is of more liberal opinions than most middle-aged matrons, but it was kind of her to call.

SHELLEY. Kind! Now don't you think Mrs Gisborne might just have been moved by curiosity, not to speak of the passing expectation of perhaps a glimpse of our illustrious... no, our infamous neighbour?

MARY. Shelley, it was very kind – !

SHELLEY. So, they can certainly tell all the English Community that no, they never saw so much as an eyelash of Lord Byron...

He runs to the terrace door and throws off the tablecloth.

...but they saw every inch of Percy Shelley, the whole natural man!

MARY. Shelley!

SHELLEY (*laughing*). Mrs Gisborne! Come back! Maria! Look at me, am I not a pretty sight? Look what the sea threw up! What? You've never seen a naked man in all your sixty summers. She's fainted, smelling salts? Come here, I'll give you a sniff of the sea.

ELISE, *the maid, enters from the terrace, exactly from where she'll have had a good view of the naked* SHELLEY. *He is laughing and unabashed, she professionally deadpan.* MARY *is not amused.*

ELISE. Madame? Shall I clear the tea things?

MARY. Yes, yes, you may, Elise, of course.

SHELLEY *is still trailing the tablecloth.*

SHELLEY. Yes, and maybe bring in the brandy, Elise.

MARY. Oh no, dearest!

ELISE. Yes, sir.

She takes the tea tray and exits again to where she's come from.

MARY. We do not take alcohol, you say yourself – !

SHELLEY. No, we have no need of intoxicants. A failure of the imagination I call it, but when we have guests –

MARY. No, Shelley, no brandy, not tonight, I don't want him to come!

SHELLEY *grabs her, spins round and hugs her in a mad dance, wrapping her up in the tablecloth too.*

SHELLEY. Do we care anything for prudish old hypocrites?

MARY. No!

SHELLEY. Prime ministers and poltickers?

MARY. No!

SHELLEY. Papas who go back on every principle they have ever published and are suddenly scandalised by love freed from the shackles of marriage? What do we care for them?

MARY. Nothing!

SHELLEY. Less than nothing. Let love know no limits!

They twirl and kiss, euphoric.

MARY. Now, go and change!

SHELLEY. Come with me, Mary.

MARY. Change!

SHELLEY. C'mon, Mary...

MARY. I have to feed William!

SHELLEY. Kiss me.

They kiss.

MARY. Your lips are cold! Oh, Shelley, you made me shiver.

They kiss again, longer. An intrusion of movement in the shadows.

Who's there?

Stillness. Silence.

SHELLEY. Nobody. It's nothing. What's the matter? Kiss me.

He kisses her again. She responds passionately. ELISE *enters with brandy on a tray, and coughs.*

ELISE. Madame…

MARY (*embarrassed*). Yes, Elise?

ELISE. Milord Byron's man, madame, he says he has come to fetch you both.

MARY (*to* SHELLEY). You go!

SHELLEY. Mary! He'll be offended…

MARY. You go with him.

SHELLEY. Mary –

MARY. I have to feed Willmouse.

SHELLEY. I'll stay with you.

MARY. Go and sail with Byron on the lake. You know you want to.

SHELLEY. Tonight I promise you I'll make you shiver, Mary.

Exit SHELLEY. *From far away, calling:*

CLAIRE. Elise! Elise!

ELISE *begins to go.* MARY *stops her.*

MARY. Oh, Elise!

ELISE. Yes, madame.

MARY. You must have thought Mr Shelley's behaviour some-what strange?

ELISE. No, madame.

MARY. Tell me, are you at home here, Elise?

ELISE *shrugs*.

ELISE. S'pose so, madame. I am at home. I was born here in Switzerland.

MARY. No, Elise, I meant... (*In a blurt.*) you must not be surprised at anything Mr Shelley does, he is... I think you know we are not, he is not bound by normal conventions, he cares nothing for them, neither of us do! But he is a good, good man, he is against all viciousness and cruelty and tyranny and ownership. What is nakedness compared to...

ELISE *withholds her reassurance. Eventually:*

ELISE (*shrugging*). It's only nature, madame.

MARY. Thank you, Elise.

ELISE. May I go, ma'am?

ELISE *begins to go again.*

MARY. Oh, Elise! Elise, in the packing today, that arrived from England, there is such a pretty shawl... and a bonnet that – yes, I'm sure – would look very fetching on you!

ELISE. Thank you, madame.

CLAIRE (*a voice still far away*). Elise! Elise, where are you, you tiresome creature? Come and help me make myself pretty!

ELISE. Can I go, madame? Mam'zelle Claire, she –

MARY. Of course you may. And do take away the brandy, please, we'll have no need of it this evening.

ELISE. Yes, ma'am.

MARY *goes to the terrace and out.* ELISE *takes up the tray with the decanter again, murmurs under her breath, but quite audibly:*

Yes, madame, no, madame, take it, leave it. A bonnet! A bonnet! Very fetching, I'm sure...

Exit ELISE.

Transition: lights change back to that opening scene, present time, again. Widow MARY, *shawled, dressing-gowned, at her desk. There's movement in the shadows again.*

MARY. We were so happy then, always, Shelley and I, even with Claire, our ever-constant companion.

CREATURE'S VOICE. You should love this. The creator should not shun his creature.

MARY. Oh, Claire Clairmont, you were always so jealous of me. Everything I had, you had to have it too. Everything...

CREATURE'S VOICE. Why? Why?

MARY. Perhaps I am unjust to her? My millstone and my sister. Since I was three years old. My papa married her mama.

'You are to be sisters now. Share your doll.' It's my doll. It's my book. I'm clever!

'You may be cleverer but I'm prettier, my mama says so. *Your* mama is dead.'

Mama. My dead mama. All the time of my growing up the legend of my dead mama. And she died giving birth to me.

Rivers of blood. I heard the cook tell the parlourmaid when she thought I wasn't listening. Puppies at her breasts so they'd suck until the afterbirth came away. No use. She died.

CREATURE'S VOICE. Who made me? Who made This...? Frankenstein.

MARY. Oh, but Claire or no Claire, we were so happy then, always, that summer, Shelley and I, before *he* came!

She actually means BYRON, *but:*

CREATURE'S VOICE. Frankenstein, why did you make me, why did you make me not beautiful?

Echo and fade. Lights change.

Back in sunlit Switzerland. CLAIRE, *in petticoats, is having her lacing done up by* ELISE, *in obedient ladies-maid mode.* ELISE *has brought* CLAIRE's *dress.*

CLAIRE *is young, radiant, overexcited.*

CLAIRE. Tight! Tighter! Lace me nice and small, Elise! Make me beautiful.

MARY *comes in from the terrace in her white muslin frock, eating an apple.*

MARY. – And breathless!

CLAIRE. Not me! Now my hair. One hundred strokes so it'll shine! Ow! Elise, you're tugging. Give it to me. Clumsy! Mary, do you not think we are somewhat alike? *Oui?* Yes, we do resemble each other after all.

MARY. How could we, we are not sisters.

CLAIRE. Not in blood, no. But we are closer perhaps than sisters, *oui*? Haven't we always shared everything?

MARY (*murmurs*). Since we were three years old…

CLAIRE. You love to write! And I love to write! You found a passionate poet to be your lover. And I –

MARY. Came with us!

CLAIRE. Mary! *Tu n'est pas gentile!* What else could I do? (*Pause.*) You are such a scarlet lady, Mary. And now I am scarlet too! We are two very scarlet ladies. Tongs, Elise!

MARY. I'm not!

ELISE. Madame. (*She passes the tongs.*)

CLAIRE. Oh yes, you are! In the world's eyes. Not hot enough, silly girl, here! (*Pause.*) Mary found herself a young and beautiful and a passionate poet to be her heart's companion. And Claire found herself a… not *quite* so young but quite as beautiful and quite as passionate a poet to be hers!

MARY. Oh, Claire, be careful!

Elise, do go fetch me that ribbon from next door, please.

ELISE goes, then – at CLAIRE, urgently:

Why, this morning at dawn I saw you running through the gap in the hedges back through the garden to the kitchen quarters, all disordered with your hair loose, losing your shoe like Cinderella –

Re-enter ELISE unseen by MARY. Stands. Listens.

And that maid presented it back to you with such an ironical little bob of a curtsey and the most insolent smirk on her face.

CLAIRE. So the servants see we too have a little blood in our veins…

ELISE. Ribbon, madame!

CLAIRE. Probably jealous, aren't you, Elise! All England would be jealous of me if they knew. All the ladies in England, at least!

MARY. Jealous! To see you make a fool of yourself, throwing yourself at a man just because he's a scandal – oh, and a famous poet!

CLAIRE. I love him. And I know he loves me. Such a scandal, though! Imagine! Peacocks, packing cases all over the quay-side, monkeys escaping from their cages, a piano dangling in mid-air. And the ladies! All the ladies weeping oceans into their cambric handkerchiefs, pressing billets-doux on him, sending little black pageboys to shower him with locks of their hair. Do you know, Mary, some ladies even cut off –

MARY. There can be only one outcome of all this, Claire! He is married already!

CLAIRE *(laughing)*. And you are an *'ippocreet!*

ELISE. Careful, Madame Claire, these tongs are very hot!

CLAIRE. Byron loathes and detests Annabel with all his heart. Byron has far less truck with Annabel after only a month or two's parting than Shelley has with his Harriet after nearly three years!

MARY. Harriet is the mother of his children. He cannot leave her destitute, his children bereft – I would not for a moment wish him to. Harriet is…

CLAIRE. His wife, *n'est ce pas*?

MARY (*gentler*). Claire, don't let's quarrel. I… I cannot bear it when we do.

CLAIRE. No. Don't let's quarrel, Mary. You are so good, of course you are not jealous. I was silly! Of course Shelley must care for Harriet. Oh, Mary! (*Kisses her.*) I want to love *you*, and Shelley and little William, and… oh, Mary, I feel as though my heart could burst. The moment I met my Albé, that very first instant –

MARY (*bursts*). Would you mother a fatherless child?

CLAIRE *wavers, won't answer for a beat, then:*

CLAIRE. Mary, you do not know how cruel my life was, *vraiment*! You had Shelley to be your protector, I had no one… I told Byron, I wrote to him… once or twice, and told him what his poetry meant to me, how reading it had transformed my whole drab existence and that made him responsible for me – for the Creator should not shun his creature – and I… (*Brazenly.*) I – yes I did! – I arranged that we would go away together and be free and unknown and we could return the following morning!

Well, did not your mama defy convention so?

I am sure she thought it shameful that women must simper and sit in the chimney corner and make mimsy mouths and wait for men to decide to kiss them. I am sure she looked forward to a time when woman as well as man may freely state her desire.

MARY. Of course! But –

CLAIRE. But what? Everything your mother ever thought, everything she wrote – Your mama wanted that women should be free.

MARY. Do you want to be a mother? Because –

CLAIRE. There is no stronger bond between a man and a woman than the making of a child. It is only nature, Mary. (*Pause.*) I think… perhaps… it may have happened already. Oh – I'm sure *not* – don't let's quarrel! You said so yourself. We mustn't quarrel. We must be happy here – the lake, the high Alps – we are a million miles away from tight little *Angleterre*! Hasn't all our luggage been unpacked yet? Elise, hasn't –

ELISE. Madame?

CLAIRE. Our *baggages*! Lord, I'm sure it seems such ages ago we packed it, and I was in such a lather of excitement – I cannot think what we'll find when we open it! Isn't it exciting?

MARY. You know I do not interest myself much in frippery!

CLAIRE. Did you pack the blue, *ma favourite*?

MARY. I can't remember…

CLAIRE. I was always jealous of that dress. Quite green over the blue! A happy dress – you wore it always that summer when we were sixteen and I was the little bird that carried messages between you and Shelley and you walked together in the graveyard.

SHELLEY *enters, for first beat of his presence a strange and frightening shape, then graceful light-footed* SHELLEY, *finger to his lips, holding a blindfold.*

CLAIRE *sees him, smiles, distracts* MARY *by tying, choker-fashion, a thin red-velvet ribbon round her throat.*

Look at me, Mary. Look! Do you not think this is fetching? It is my latest fashion… oh, rather an antique one to be sure, but then something genuinely flattering is surely *à la mode* for all time… The brave beldams of the French revolution affected it. The thinnest simple crimson-velvet ribbon at the throat… '*À la victime*'! (*She laughs*.) – Don't you love that?

So witty! Such a piquant bit of stylishness. Oh, only a fashion, Mary, but I'm sure the gentlemen will love it!

SHELLEY, *giggling his high-pitched laugh, grabs* MARY *and ties the blindfold over her eyes. She gets a fright but* SHELLEY *and* CLAIRE *begin an at first sweet, childish and innocent 'Blind Man's Buff', calling* MARY *in different voices and dodging under her arms and giggling.* MARY *tries to join in as if it's fun. But soon she's spinning round, grasping, stumbles towards, stops at* ELISE, *who has been standing silent at the edge of the game, an onlooker.*

MARY *feels all down* ELISE'*s face and shoulders and breasts.*

MARY. Claire?

CLAIRE. Not I!

Then she feels who it is and screams slightly.

CLAIRE *and* SHELLEY *are laughing aloud.*

(*From elsewhere*.) You're getting colder!

MARY (*spinning around*). Shelley!

CLAIRE. Getting cold-er! That was only the maid, Mary, and she's not in our game!

MARY (*grasping, desperate*). Shelley!

Giggling, SHELLEY *and* CLAIRE *dodge her, pull* ELISE *out from her grasp too. The game goes on so till:*

BYRON *limps in silently.* MARY *bumps into him, touching, and then she grasps him, hugging. Holds on.*

Shelley! Oh, darling, free me –

BYRON *kisses her lightly on the cheek and unties her blindfold.*

BYRON. Easily… but it's only me, Mary.

MARY *looks confused, turns away.*

ELISE *helps a suddenly imperious* CLAIRE *into her dress.*

CLAIRE. Byron! Where have you been? I was waiting! When my Albé says he will come over with the poem he wishes me to transpose then I *do* expect him to come.

BYRON. But I didn't.

Ah! Such a fine sail we had, eh, Shelley? We'll get you your sea legs yet, Shiloh! I was as good as born with them. (*He limps arrogantly across the room.*) It's dry land I find difficult, except when I have strong drink taken and am half-seas-over. Well, ladies, how have you been wiling away the idle hours? Apart from rouging, titivating and bathing in asses' milk and waiting for your sailor boys to return?

CLAIRE *twirls around before him.*

CLAIRE. And don't we look pretty? Albé, don't you admire my necklace?

BYRON. Very diverting, yes. Not so bonny as that gewgaw you wear at your throat, though, Mary. And who is that?

CLAIRE. That's Mary's famous mama!

BYRON *looks at it, holding* MARY *by it close to him.*

BYRON. The writer, eh? She was bonny, but not so bonny as you.

MARY. I do not resemble her.

BYRON. No, she was all russet – fire and earth. You're more… water and air.

MARY *pulls away.*

MARY. And where's Polidori? He doesn't join us this evening?

SHELLEY. Pollydolly says he won't come. I think he's jealous.

BYRON (*laughing at the idea of it*). He says he's busy writing…

MARY. He has never refused to join us before…

SHELLEY. The wild eye, the pale brow, the fevered scratchings and scribblings! (*He laughs.*) A harsh mistress he's taken up with, the Muse, she'll lead him a merry dance, if she don't desert him like she has me these days and nights…

CLAIRE. Shall I go, Albé? I'll charm him into joining us. I'll tell him it won't be the same without him.

BYRON. Without his French volume of ghost stories more likely! Lord, but there are some stirring tales in that book of his – oh, after what you read aloud to us last night, Mary Godwin, all the long night through I slept scarce a wink. Yes, after our… little *soirée*, our cosy little *conversazione* of the supernatural…

SHELLEY (*playful, in a mock-sepulchral voice*). Once upon a time, there was Byron and Mary, and Claire and Shelley. It was a dark and a moonless night –

BYRON. – and all night long I was quite unmanned and unnerved by thoughts of a light pale little girl with silken hair and the strangest stories to tell. All I could see was Mary, Mary…

SHELLEY *is laughing.*

MARY *is held in thrall, but horrified.*

CLAIRE *is jealous, but when, pouting, she goes to try and hang around* BYRON*'s neck, she is shrugged off.*

BYRON *never flinches from his blatant attention to* MARY.

SHELLEY. See, Mary, you are a witch, cast quite a spell on poor old Byron here!

BYRON. Ask poor Pollydolly! I had to summon him in the middle of the night and he had to administer me the strongest draught to make me… lie down and get me to sleep.

Well, dear friends, and shall we eat dinner soon, I'm ravenous. Where's the maid? She's always forgetting to bring the bloody decanter! Elise! Elise! Lord, I am so hungry I could eat a Scotch reviewer. Roasted. Couldn't you? Oh, I forgot, the Shelley's are Utopian vegetarians who won't gorge themselves on anything bloodier than an orange, eh?

ELISE *enters*.

Bring us brandy, my dear, did not you know I was arrived?

ELISE. Yes, sir.

BYRON. Well, surely by now you know how to fulfil my every sensual desire and pleasure?

ELISE. Yes, sir. (*Confused*.) No, sir…

BYRON. Well, just bring the bloody brandy on the double. 'Twould be a start…

ELISE. Yes, sir…

ELISE *exits*.

MARY. Lord Byron! Please don't –

SHELLEY *sees that* MARY*'s really angry, is outraged at* BYRON*'s proprietorial attitude to her servant, and he interrupts, tries to change the subject.*

SHELLEY. Ah, Mary, I wish you had come with us… Today we were right inside that storm, I was part of it.

MARY. I am afraid to sail.

SHELLEY. Nonsense, Mary, you *want* to. I know you do! Remember back there in St Pancras Graveyard we used to blow bubbles and sail paper boats, and plan how we would sail away for ever.

BYRON. Graveyard? That does not sound the most romantic sport for courtship, still –

CLAIRE. That was Mary's secret place. Her mother's grave. She would tell me how her mother would come and haunt me. I never went there.

MARY (*heartfelt*). There, I could be perfectly alone.

CLAIRE. Alone until you began to encourage Shelley to accompany you!

SHELLEY. And I needed little encouragement! (*Kisses* MARY.) You know, Byron, I was half in love with Mary before I even met her. I'd go to Godwin's house. And how I worshipped that man –

CLAIRE. You used to bring Harriet!

SHELLEY. Sometimes.

CLAIRE *turns to* MARY.

CLAIRE. You were away in Scotland then. *My* mama found you unmanageable!

MARY. I was just fifteen! She sent me away!

SHELLEY. I could not wait to see the daughter of this excellent man I wished was my father!

CLAIRE. That would have made Mary your sister!

SHELLEY. My soul's sister. She is. Has been always!

CLAIRE. If she was your real sister you could not –

BYRON (*laughing*). Not without being the storm in every teacup in Albion – and you may take that from the horse's mouth! Godwin, eh? *Political Justice*!

SHELLEY. The best and bravest and most important book ever written in the English language.

BYRON. High praise!

SHELLEY. Not exaggerated!

BYRON. Poor Mary-Mary! Wearing her mother round her neck and her father on her sleeve.

SHELLEY. Albé, I defy anyone to read that book and not be filled with the certainty that, as sound politics diffuse through society – as they inevitably will – freedom and justice for both men and women then must be universal.

BYRON *laughs*.

BYRON. And do you think I have not read Godwin's great work? Well, I have read it, when it was fashionable – long before you, Mary, were out of schoolroom pinafores, I had seen that silly book for the euphoric bombast it was.

ELISE *enters with the decanter.*

Ah, Elise, come here. Elise, come help us, we need you to demonstrate.

ELISE *curtseys*.

ELISE. Lord Byron.

BYRON. What do you do, Elise?

ELISE. Sir?

BYRON. For a livelihood, Elise. Who are you?

ELISE. Mrs Shelley's maid, sir.

BYRON. A maid?

ELISE. Yes, sir.

BYRON (*indicating* MARY). Well, Mademoiselle Maid, and who is this?

ELISE. Mrs Shelley, sir.

BYRON. No, indeed, it is not! This is – a Great Man. A… philosopher, let's say.

ELISE. Sir?

BYRON. No one reads him, of course. Can you read?

ELISE. Yes, sir.

BYRON (*amazed*). You can?

ELISE. I'm learning, sir. A little each day. Mrs Shelley, she helps me when William is asleep, and Mr Shelley, sir.

BYRON. He does?

ELISE. In the afternoons, sir. Sometimes.

BYRON. A maid who can read!

ELISE. And write, sir. Mrs Shelley helps me to form my letters…

BYRON. Perhaps we shall have dogs on two legs next, entering the House of Lords, and pissing on its portals.

SHELLEY. Better than wolves and vipers and crocodiles that we have to contend with currently!

BYRON. Indeed! But we digress! Elise, who is this?

ELISE. A… philosopher, sir.

BYRON. And who are you?

ELISE. A maid.

BYRON. His maid.

ELISE (*very uncomfortably*). Yes, sir.

BYRON. And now I have to decide which one of you to save.

MARY. Byron, this is an abuse – Elise, don't be alarmed, this is but a game of our neighbour's, he –

BYRON. Wishes to demonstrate a philosophical argument of the illustrious Godwin's. And do you know who Godwin is, Elise?

ELISE. He is… Mrs Shelley's father, sir?

BYRON. Indeed. Mary Godwin's famous father. And now we shall examine his concept of justice, ladies and gentlemen! You are both in a burning building and I have to decide which of you to save. Can't you feel the flames catch at your petticoats, lick at your ankles?

ELISE *looks down. She is angry, silent, impotent.*

Can't you feel the thick smoke choke you? Elise, can't you?
Answer me, girl!

ELISE. Yes, sir.

BYRON. Now I am concerned with justice. Godwin's justice.

There is an old maxim, everyone's heard of it, although only
you, Claire Clairmont, seem inclined to put it into practice
around here: that we should love our neighbour as ourselves.

CLAIRE (*going to his side*). Albé!

BYRON. Keep seated! I'm on the track of justice. You, philosopher, and you, chambermaid, are presumed of equal worth.
You are both human beings, are you not?

And entitled to equal attention... in the natural world at any
rate. As a general principle? Yes? No? And yet Godwin says
I must save –

MARY. Well, I understand why my father advocated the saving
of me.

BYRON. The philosopher!

MARY. Yes. There is the consideration that the common good
of all mankind for all time will benefit from my work. So
save me.

SHELLEY. Bravo, Mary!

BYRON. Ah, but suppose this mere maid were my wife? Or my
mother? Yes, or my sister? Certainly I should want to save
my beloved sister before some old philosopher.

MARY. My wife, my sister, my mother! What is so magical
about the pronoun 'my'? My sister may be a fool... or a
harlot... If she be, then what worth is she lent by the fact she
is my sister?

BYRON. Where is your heart, Mary? Hear that, Elise? Are you
listening, Claire? She'd consign her own sister to the flames.

But I don't know I believe her. I think it's Godwin's daughter wishing to convince us – and her papa – that she has her head in the right place!

MARY. Suppose I were myself the philosopher's maid, I should choose to die rather than him.

BYRON. Ah, so you won't grant life to the maid. Elise, tell me who are you going to save? Yourself, or Mister Philosopher?

ELISE. I... I shouldn't like to say, sir.

BYRON. Come, Elise, you are among friends, you can tell us what you think.

ELISE. What would you like me to say, sir?

BYRON. Tell us the truth. Who would you save?

ELISE. I should save myself, sir.

BYRON *bursts out laughing.*

BYRON. Thank you, Elise, that is what I wished to hear.

ELISE. May I go, madame?

MARY. Yes, Elise.

ELISE. Madame, I did not mean... I hope I did not say the wrong thing, madame?

MARY. You are a good girl, Elise.

ELISE. Thank you, madame.

ELISE *exits.*

MARY. It was wicked of us to use her so.

BYRON. Why? She is but a maid.

MARY. But I have not bought the right to abuse her. I ought to act towards all creatures with benevolence.

BYRON. Benevolence by all means, Mrs Shelley. Nicety costs nothing. But recognise that where you are paymaster, benevolence is yours to bestow... or to take away.

SHELLEY. Peddling in human flesh... a vile and a universal thing. To be born poor may be translated: to be born a slave. The lot of the working people! In the new hells of our cities, the mechanic himself becomes a sort of machine. His limbs and articulations are converted into wood and wires.

Surely they must rise up, they shall rise up.

MARY. But Elise is not my puppet. It is my duty to educate her, enlighten her.

BYRON. So she can see the justice of her giving up her own life for you! No, she is not your puppet, Mary. Thank God we may own the body but, although we stuff the head with Latin, algebra and Platonics, we cannot own the heart. (*Pause.*) Nevertheless, if I am honest, and I think I am, I must admit that possession of the odd body does all but suffice. For me. But then I'm no Godwinite. I won't tyrannise the world by force-feeding it freedom.

CLAIRE. I don't like these games, I wish Pollydolly was here.

BYRON. Well, he's not. So we have to otherwise divert ourselves. Pollydolly! Pollydolly, indeed. Honestly, Shelley, I pick me as travelling companion a physician – hoping he can at once apply the pharmaceutical leeches *and* keep the human ones at bay – and what does he do but decide he should forsake his doctoring and take up competing with *me* – and you – at the scribbling. Ah, the Literary Life! And truly, Claire, I think, he *is* a little jealous! Since I found myself such... congenial neighbours and stimulating companions I have little time for Pollydolly. (*He kisses CLAIRE lightly, sarcastically.*) I fear we have begun to tire of one another. Oh, is it not the way of all human intimacy?

Even the best of marriages, you know yourself, Shelley, grows tedious to the combatants.

And even the firmest friendships come unstuck...

CLAIRE. 'True love *differs* from gold and clay. To divide is not to take away.' Shelley's poem, Albé! Remember?

BYRON. Pretty lines!

MARY. It's true! Because... because Shelley loves me, it does not mean he must stop loving Harriet; I should be wrong to wish him to.

SHELLEY. I think if she would only consent to meet Mary she would become her friend.

BYRON. Honestly, Shelley, you do take the Bath bun and the biscuit too! (*He laughs.*) I'm afraid you're not for this world. Shiloh! Love is all on account, debits, debits, precious few credits, and always less in the coffers than one thinks there is – a sudden running-out and not a ha'p'worth left is the common way to the inevitable bankruptcy.

The worst of Annabel's lies and slanders is I'll see her in hell. If only she'd keep a virtuous silence she'd gain the other place, and eternity were not too long a time I'd never see her again...

SHELLEY. There could not have been devised anything – anything! – more hostile to human happiness than marriage.

CLAIRE. Amen!

BYRON. I'll drink to that!

BYRON *polishes off the last drop in his glass.*

SHELLEY. Abolish marriage, then all connections between women and men will be natural. And right – because choice and change will be possible – will even be desired by both!

The two women cheer and applaud SHELLEY. MARY *goes to him.*

BYRON. Lord, Shiloh, I'm not much of a one for such airy Platonics. I am a simple man. Ladies, I am as ditchwater dull and tethered to the earth as clodhopper Caliban... I am happy as a pig in... the proverbial acorn wood. I'll gobble up the lot. Shelley here, though, he's a different kettle of nightingales. Oh, we only have to look at him and we dissolve. He's all Light and Grace, is Shiloh! He's Ariel, a pure spirit moving through the changing air, fashioning liquid verse into new forms for freedom. How he will flame and amaze! And how about you Miranda-Mary?

Friends, how shall we amuse ourselves?

Oh, to hell with Dr Polidori and his German volume of *Fantasmagoriana*! Listen, I'll set us a little contest. Why should we content ourselves with translated, traditional horrors, all bookish and stilted. Home-grown ones are the best. We shall all write a ghost story!

CLAIRE. A story!

She laughs uproariously, clapping her hands, dancing around in circles.

A story, a story! Who can write the most horrid tale! Oh yes, we shall all be terrorists – Claire will, and Mary will, and Shelley will, and Byron, and Claire and Shelley and Byron and Mary…

And fade out and lights change.

Back to widow MARY, *who is back at her writing desk, suffering as she remembers.*

MARY. I did not want to write –

CREATURE'S VOICE. Did I request thee, Maker, from my clay to mould me?

MARY. I did not want to write. I did not want to write. Daughter of *Political Justice*, daughter of *A Vindication of the Rights of Woman*. And I wrote you. If I had known the misery, the terror, the grief I foretold for myself? I did not want to write you anyway. Nothing came to me, no ideas, I was empty. Everybody was engaged on his creation, except me.

Back to Switzerland, 1816 again, a few days later, and much later at night, with the wind outside, summer storms. BYRON *and* SHELLEY *with opium pipes.*

The trio of BYRON, SHELLEY *and* CLAIRE *are all writing.*

SHELLEY (*deep in thought*)....A beautiful creature, half-man, half-woman. Perfect, therefore terrifying!... (*Writes.*)

BYRON. There's Mad Shelley, and Bad Byron, and Sad Polidori next door, scribbling away like a dervish, muttering 'Vampyre, vampyre.' Why, even *Glad*-eyed Claire is lusting somewhat after cuttlefish ink and quill pens, eh, Claire?

CLAIRE. I tell you, I have begun one.

BYRON. Of course you have. (*Mutters.*) It'd be too much to hope, would it, that girls of eighteen had nought but fertile imaginations...

MARY *comes in to join them.*

And how about you, Mary, have you begun yours?

SHELLEY. Is he asleep at last?

MARY. He's sleeping.

CLAIRE. You should let the maid! Don't they say 'tis a pity to spoil the creatures?

MARY. When you are a mother, Claire, perhaps I'll listen to your advice.

BYRON. Ah! (*Mutters.*) And this may be sooner than you think, apparently...

Never mind. Writing time! The Contest! Creation! I asked you, Mary, how goes your story?

SHELLEY (*bursting out enthusiastically*). Well, all I'll say of mine – it's scarce begun, to tell the truth – but I will say it's something about a dream.

BYRON. A dream, eh? Marvellous! How about you, Mary?

SHELLEY. A dream of a beautiful creature – half-man, half-woman – who lives high, high, on the topmost pinnacle above that awful ravine, where naked power, dressed as a river, pours out of the rock, and down... Remember, Albé, when we finally reached the source of the Arve?

BYRON. Up mountain and glacier! No wonder we're chilled and stiff and ache so that Polidori had to lard us with liniment. Ladies, I'm sure we reek like racehorses...

SHELLEY. It wasn't a river. It was pure, naked, absolute Power. That element. Oh, in the disguise of a river! This time.

The surfaces of things hide from us what they truly are.

MARY *is thrilled by this,* BYRON *laughing at it.*

MARY. Oh yes! The surfaces... of things... hide from us what they really are!

SHELLEY. The same secret strength of things flows through us all, making us work. Just because it's invisible doesn't mean it isn't real...

Think of us! We four.

Oh, there are wires and bonds between us that are as fine-spun as filigree and as intricately structured as a spider's web and stronger than blood – or Manchester iron.

As imperative as the delicate smells that drag the insect to the nectar.

BYRON. Gossamer, blood, pig-iron and stink! Four very different things in my book.

MARY. Then what's in your book, Albé, is only the tip of the iceberg.

BYRON. Ah, Mary! Brave new world that has such poets in it.

BYRON *drinks to her, toasting her.*

SHELLEY *begins to write again, almost in a trance, staring. A moment or two's silence but for the scratching of the pen nibs.*

I'm asking you, Mary Godwin –

MARY. What?

BYRON. Have you started your story?

MARY. I don't think we would play with such dangerous
things.

BYRON. Won't dabble in the dark?

MARY. There is no darkness! There are no forces of evil
outside of ourselves. Once we let the clear light of reason
sear through… Besides, how can I write when William
screams all day?

BYRON. As Claire said, let the nursemaid see to him.

SHELLEY. Naked!

MARY. He needs me, every child needs his mother.

> BYRON *notices* SHELLEY, *who's really spooking himself,
> writing and muttering.*

SHELLEY. Naked! Naked! God! And eyes…

BYRON. *Fan… tas… magor… iana…*! What was that story,
Mary? You read it last night. 'And when the moon…' What?
'And by that…' What, Mary?

MARY. Blue and baleful light.

BYRON. 'Blue and baleful light!'

> Shelley! Shelley! Does she not make your flesh to creep and
> your gorge to rise? Oh, I know she does mine! 'He saw that
> in his arms…' yes?

> MARY *is almost in a trance now,* BYRON*'s power has her
> half-hypnotised – she can't not answer.*

MARY. 'He saw that in his arms he clasped the pale, pale ghost
of her he had deserted.'

SHELLEY. No! Who in hell are you? Mary! Not-Mary! Your
breasts… you have eyes, eyes in your breasts… don't stare at
me! Keep… her away from me!

MARY. Shelley –

But he screams, runs from her. Chaos. BYRON *tries to hold*
SHELLEY *in the room,* CLAIRE *begins fighting with*
BYRON *to let* SHELLEY *escape.*

CLAIRE. Let him go! Leave him! Mary! Albé! Help him!

SHELLEY *breaks loose and runs screaming from the room.*

MARY *stands, upset, unable to move.*

Shelley? Hush, Shelley, it's me, your Claire, calm, I'm coming!

CLAIRE *runs out after him.* BYRON *stands stock-still*
looking at MARY, *she at him.* BYRON *shrugs.*

BYRON. He reads too much.

MARY *belatedly makes to follow* SHELLEY.

MARY. Shelley...!

BYRON *stops her by grabbing her wrist.*

BYRON. No, Mary, let Claire. You are not the right person. You
are the subject of his... Waking Nightmare.

MARY. I must go to him. We always have avoided stimulants.
Even alcohol, especially alcohol, as well you know! Too
much opium...

BYRON. Too much imagination. Let Claire see to him. Claire
will calm him.

BYRON *lets* MARY's *arm go. She stays.*

MARY. I must go to my husband.

BYRON. Ah? Strange, but I thought poor Shiloh had a wife
already! Mary, Mary, don't scuttle off like a manhandled
maidservant! Don't spurn my company. Lord knows, I've
had enough of ostracism in England.

Well, well, I should have honestly thought it impossible to
scandalise Shelley, the Anti-Christ's Lady! The Queen of the
Ménage à Trois!

MARY. What do you mean?

BYRON. Was not... What's-his-name, your dear friend, Mary?

MARY (*involuntarily*)....Hogg?

BYRON. Yes, Hogg. Thomas Jefferson Hogg. Percy Bysshe Shelley's bosom companion. And his rival in love for the affections of their 'participated pleasure' – Mary Wollstonecraft Godwin!

MARY. Hogg was a brother to me...

BYRON. Ah! Fraternal love! I've heard of such things.

MARY. Surely Shelley did not trust you with such a secret?

BYRON. Hush-hush, of course not. Claire did, didn't she – now, it was not unkindly meant, oh, don't break my confidence to you and chide her. It was in an unguarded, not to say unclothed moment...

MARY. You cannot know how cruel you are! He was Shelley's friend. Shelley and I don't believe in... I wanted to show Shelley I felt the same as he did about freedom.

BYRON. Goodness, Mary, what's to get in such a tush about? If you loved Hogg, what's to shock? Surely it was nothing more than the revolutionaries declaring independence from the laws the rest of us humble mortals have to live by – or some of us frolic to flout! Surely it was merely the embracing of your own published principles, Mary Godwin?

MARY. How could a libertine like you understand? It was a noble experiment!

BYRON. The dissection of the affections! The analytical, anatomical dismantling of the human heart!

MARY. We wanted a new way to live. Can't you understand that?

BYRON. Oh yes... Intellectually I can conceive of it, Mrs Shelley. But there is something hideously unnatural in such a cold-blooded, put-together passion, is there not? I cannot believe it can have been a very pretty thing in practice. And I'm all for practice... making perfect.

Mary! Mary, I am a simple soul at heart! None of your rational splits between the heart and the head for me. None of your cold-blooded laboratories of sexual relations, just the head, the heart, the body and soul!

MARY. You have no soul!

BYRON. – The healthy mind in the healthy body! But I do have a soul, Mary. A blackened, burnt-out cinder of a soul perhaps, may it rot in hell. And it has done, it has done.

Don't say you've swallowed Shelley's fallacy of free-thinking? So, you're free to agree with your Atheist, allowed to assent to uniting yourself with your Dissenting Angel...

But I, Mary, am like all blasphemers, a true believer! A libertine who breaks the code, but is good and glad it exists to rupture. The Lord knows, were it not for legitimate married love, there would not be a convention worth outraging!

MARY. You are a heartless seducer!

BYRON. Not heartless, just... faint-hearted sometimes. Where it could really... make a difference. Oh, I do tumble the occasional dollymop, that I do freely admit, do the odd bit of hobnobbing below stairs, and below the greasy petticoats of scrubbing scullery wenches – I'm not snobbish!

But it's all just to kill time, Mary.

MARY. Are you trying to make me pity you? For –

BYRON. Not at all! No, Mary, it is not that I am half-hearted in my love affairs. Just that recently... Well, you know all about that, all England knows all about that... recently I have been rather half-witted about who I chose – but do we ever really *choose* who we truly love?

MARY. Your sister!

BYRON. *Half*-sister, Mrs Shelley. But yes, I love my sister Augusta. Too much to subject that love to the warpings of Platonics. Frustrated love perverts, produces monsters! But as for you, Mary, and Shelley, and Hogg, and Claire, with your frigged-up intellectual *notions* of passion!

Oh, it is not love which is dead in my heart, Mary, but hope merely.

Like all highly coloured comedians, I do take a dim view of the world.

MARY. And that is your real sin, Lord Byron. You do… give up too easily!

BYRON. Do I? You mean if I but bide my time, bonny Mary…?

MARY. I mean you give way to pessimism! It is unforgivable! How can you, in a century which has given us Arkwright… and Owen… and Watt…

MARY *and* BYRON. The French Revolution?

BYRON. And the Terror, the heads bounding into baskets, the Jacobins, the Girondins, the Sans-Culottes, the Ruin, the Rot, the Reaction! Did not Sweet Shelley's second honeymoon straddle the charred and blackened corpse of La Belle France? Or didn't he notice? Or didn't you notice, Mary-Mary?

MARY. Our eyes were wide open! My Shelley's no sleepwalking dreamer. He was the first, the only one of his generation quickly to see through Napoleon!

BYRON. Bravo!

MARY. My mother, did you know she travelled to France during the Revolution, she lived in Paris all during…

BYRON. That bloodbath?

MARY. Yes! And she did not give up hope.

BYRON. Mary Wollstonecraft's Cookbook: 'You cannot make an omelette without cracking a few skulls.' Percy Bysshe Shelley's Dreambook: 'It's getting a little better all the time!'

MARY. And should a true poet like Shelley not indulge in dreams and aspirations?

BYRON. Humbug and bubbles, Mrs Shelley! Mary, you are getting good and sick, I know it, of Ariel's head-in-the-clouds hopefulness. Come on, come down to earth where you belong! Come on, come and curl up with old club-footed Caliban!

Hold for a long moment. Till it almost looks as if she will. She steps a step closer to him. He flicks at her mother's pendant on her throat.

Come, write that story, and let me tell you, it won't be made of nebulous ideas, pretty philosophies and pointless, pointless politics!

Everything I write is a Creature who can only live by what he sees, hears, smells, tastes, touches, and grabs, Mrs Shelley. And rather than have him starved and skinny, living on air, I'd have him rich and fat with facts, facts, facts. And any plain fact looked at without flinching is funny. At any rate, one has to laugh. Or doesn't this one? Don't you, Mary? I look at you, Mary, and I see someone who is holding it all within. A lovely lady who yet suppresses every gust, every gale, every giggle. Don't sit on your wit, just to please Shelley.

MARY. 'Like a sword without a scabbard, it wounds the wearer!' What good does wit do a woman? Wit in a woman is always sour.

BYRON. So is my sour wit womanish?

I think *not*, Mary. (*Whispers.*) I'll prove it to you...

CLAIRE enters. He hears her and turns.

We'll have Claire here sign an affidavit! Claire, come here! Kiss me.

She does. BYRON *kisses her fully and lewdly on the lips.*

Lord, Lord, I think I have found me Polidori's Vampyre!

You know, Claire, Mary's virtue is much affronted that there is so much… to-ing and fro-ing between your villa and mine. She does not like to be too near the foul sty or the hot breath of the two-backed beast!

He kisses her again, grabbing her breasts and buttocks and pulling up her skirt.

CLAIRE. Albé! Stop! Stop it! Mary's here.

BYRON. Not alone, are we not Mam'zelle Clairmont, and me so mad with lust for you?

CLAIRE. Albé, I mean it, I'm getting vexed! (*To* MARY.) Polidori came and gave him a sleeping draught. He says we're wicked, winding each other up so tightly, exciting ourselves so. We'll forget all this happened. Come away, Albé! It'll all be better in the morning. Come –

BYRON. Goodnight, Mrs Shelley.

BYRON *chases* CLAIRE *across the stage, catching her, kissing her, laughing, making her shriek. They exit.*

Lights change.

Back to widow MARY *at her desk, remembering.*

MARY. Cold. Cold and lonely. I thought: 'Go to him, go to Shelley… no! He should come to me!' I was as far away from him that night… and him only asleep next door, wound round in laudanum dreams and brandy fumes, and poppy scents of incense. But I was as far away from him as I am now. And him drowned and dead for ever.

I lay down. Not to sleep, I did not sleep, nor could I have been said to dream. Not dreaming… I saw him!

The CREATURE's *music begins, a slow throb. She senses him behind her, but does not turn round.*

The form he takes – if he is indeed made visible – is shadowy and barely lit.

She goes slowly to and lies down flat on the chaise longue, lies on it as if she is the created one, limp and lifeless. Her eyes are shut. Only her lips move, slowly.

I see him! A pale student of unhallowed arts, kneeling beside the thing he has put together.

Flash of lightning. MARY *sits up as if electrified, speaks out:*

It lives! The artist is terrified, and would rush away from his handiwork, horror-stricken. Begins to hope that, left to itself, the spark of life will fade.

Sleeps a deep and dreamless sleep. Awakens.

Behold, standing right by my bedside, looking down at me with yellow, watery, but hungry eyes...

CREATURE'S VOICE. Cry hallelujah, Frankenstein! Sing out. For you have found this, this has found you. It is easy, describe what haunts you. Frankenstein, you have thought of a story. Mary Shelley, you have seized the spark of life. Now write this.

MARY *goes to the desk begins to write.* MARY *writing, the* CREATURE'S VOICE *and* MARY*'s voice together –*

CREATURE'S VOICE *and* MARY. It was on a dreary night in November, that I beheld the accomplishment of my toils.

End of Act One.

ACT TWO

Widow MARY *with candle, quill, at her writing desk again. She has some letters, opens one, reads. Paces, frets.*

MARY. Oh, Percy Florence Shelley, my sweet son, how am I to keep you?

When your grandpapa Godwin, far from supporting us financially, asks us for money just as constantly as he did when Shelley was alive?

And when your grandpapa Shelley threatens he will cut us off without a penny if we bring out your father's poetic productions posthumous before the world and add, in his eyes, yet more infamy to the family name?

But he should know it. I will collect and edit and bring out in a single volume the works of Percy Bysshe Shelley if it is the last thing I do.

Must write!

When creation goes dead and dull, that's the time the author has to force himself to put the long hours in and have the faith that sometime soon the spark surely will return.

The Last Man, oh, Mrs Shelley – if you can but keep your courage – *this* is the book that will make your name, your fame and your fortune.

'The year is 2073, a slowly spreading plague threatens the very existence of human life on earth. Vernay, the hero of our tale –

The Last Man.'

I'll live here lonelier than the last woman alive on earth and I'll write it.

It is so much better an idea than any I ever have had before in all my life.

As for my last monstrosity, my grotesque invention, my scandal, to my surprise my enduring and popular success, no, I didn't invent you, I didn't write you, you came unbidden and I wrote you down.

Movement in the shadows.

CREATURE'S VOICE. Wrap yourself in furs, Frankenstein, for soon such ice and cold. No escape, except by the death of you or this.

MARY. I could never think how to kill you. Night after night, I had done with you, only for you to rise again.

I buried you in an avalanche, I had you leap into the smoking crater of a volcano, I burned you to death in a church.

I did not think of drowning you in the ocean...

I mangled you in the workings of a gigantic mill...

I froze you to death in an Arctic storm. But you would not die.

CREATURE'S VOICE. Come, pursue This, chase This, till This shall catch you...

MARY *picks up the volume,* Frankenstein, *opens it at random and reads with a shudder.*

MARY. 'How can I describe my emotions at this catastrophe, or how delineate the wretch which, with such infinite care I had endeavoured to form? His lips were in proportion, and I had selected his features as beautiful. *Beautiful!* Great God! His yellow skin scarcely covered the work of muscles and arteries beneath; his hair was lustrous and flowing, his teeth of a pearly whiteness – these luxuriances merely a more horrid contrast with the watery eyes, that seemed almost the same colour as the dun-white sockets in which they were set... his shrivelled complexion and straight black lips... I could not endure the aspect of the being I had created.'

CREATURE'S VOICE. Frankenstein's Frankenstein? Why did you make me? This must know.

MARY. Frankenstein's Frankenstein? Am I? I am! My God! Oh, had I known…

I am responsible.

'It was on a dreary night in November.'

I wrote that, on a stormy night in June. I was happy then, we were all of us happy then. My most congenial companions and I…

They *were* my most beloved congenial companions. Most of the time. And if they were not always… then that is my fault, surely?

'It was on a dreary night in November.'

The book I started on the shores of Lake Geneva that stormy night in June stole me away from the others. Six months later, I was still writing it.

Oh, let the baby cry!

We were back in England then, Shelley and I – with Claire.

It was on a dreary night in December…

Lights change. The desk at which MARY *writes is now in England, December 1816.*

(*The transitions into past time in Act Two happen in an even more fluid fashion.*)

Now CLAIRE *comes; very, very heavily pregnant and bored.*

CLAIRE. Oh, Mary, there you are, still scribbling? Shelley might be back from London soon. Come and I'll crimp your hair for you. Come and I'll make you beautiful for your lover coming home.

MARY. Is that what you've been doing?

CLAIRE. Making myself beautiful for my lover?

MARY. Crimping your hair!

CLAIRE. There's no point in me trying to look pretty in this condition. This kicks! Little monster! Honestly, wouldn't you think there'd be some other way, some better way? No wonder men recoil in horror when they see what they've done! So ugly!

MARY. You're not ugly. How can something so natural be ugly?

CLAIRE. It's ugly!

MARY. Shelley doesn't think it's ugly. Before William was born, when I was first pregnant, with my little girl that died… he used to hold the great globe of my belly as if it were the whole world, and press his face against it.

CLAIRE. Shelley, though, is a man in a million.

Imagine loving a big fat swollen woman!

MARY *is trying to go on writing.* CLAIRE *is lumbering about, bored and clumsy, looking out of the window.*

It has rained and rained for three days and nights without stopping. Not a glimmer in the grey sky. And all the flat sodden grey fields just soak it all up! I hate England. I hate the winter. Why did we come back here?

MARY. Because.

CLAIRE. Yes, I know, but why did the summer have to end?

Silence. MARY *gets another sentence, half-sentence done, crosses it out, scratching her pen.*

I can't even go out! All the villagers whispering about me behind my back, going in and locking their doors. Anyone would think they'd never seen a pregnant woman before.

MARY. They talk about me too! And Shelley. They don't understand, so they gossip.

CLAIRE. You don't care! All you've wanted to do ever since we came home is bury yourself in your damned book! Everything's flat around here. Except my belly.

What are you writing anyway?

Mmm?

CLAIRE *snatches a page.* MARY *tries to grab it.* CLAIRE *avoids her, reading from the manuscript:*

'His yellow skin... the work of muscles and arteries beneath; his hair was lust... his teeth of a pearly whiteness... more horrid contrast with watery eyes... shrivelled complexion and straight black lips.'

God, Mary, what a truly hideous imagination you have. Where do you get it?

MARY. Give it back!

CLAIRE *dodges* MARY, *reads lucidly another passage:*

CLAIRE. 'Here then, I retreated and lay down, happy to have found a shelter, however miserable, from the inclemency of the season and still more from the barbarity of man.' Quite!

MARY. Claire...

CLAIRE. Why didn't I stay there?

MARY. Where?

CLAIRE. In Europe. And follow him? Once his son is born, and I could say: 'Look, here is what we made together... that night we made love in the storm.'

MARY. How do you know it'll be a son?

CLAIRE. Oh, I know. Just as clearly as, that night... I know he loved me!

MARY. Oh, Claire...

CLAIRE. Boring, flat old England. Why did we come back?

MARY. Money.

CLAIRE. Yes, but why did Shelley go to London and leave us here?

MARY. Money.

Silence. MARY *writes, having pointedly taken the sheet of filched paper back from* CLAIRE. *The baby begins to cry.*

CLAIRE. Baby's crying. Ma-ma, Ba-ba wants you! I'll get him, you're too busy.

CLAIRE *comes back with the crying baby, rocking him in her arms.*

There, Willmouse pet. Ssh, where's a lamb? There's your mummy. Mama doesn't love him, does she? Not properly. Mama loves her dream child better, hmm?

Who wants Auntie Claire to give him a little brother to play with?

MARY. Cousin.

CLAIRE. Cousin, brother, what's the difference round here? Oh… Mary… sometimes I'm so frightened.

MARY. What's the use of being frightened?

CLAIRE. Is it terribly, terribly sore?

MARY. It's a pain that one forgets.

SHELLEY, *crying, bursts into the room. He is dishevelled, sobbing.* MARY *leaps to her feet.*

Dear God, Shelley, look what you made me do!

Spilt ink!

She holds up a page stained with red ink like blood.

SHELLEY *is sobbing his distress, and holds out a copy of* The Times, *December 1816.*

CLAIRE. What is it? What is in the newspaper?

MARY. Give it to me!

SHELLEY. No!

CLAIRE *grabs it, reads*.

CLAIRE. 'Tuesday December 10th... Mrs Harriet Shelley, a respectable female far advanced in pregnancy, was taken from the Serpentine River and brought home to her residence in Queen Street, Brompton, having been missed for nearly six weeks... She had a valuable ring on her finger, a want of honour in her own conduct is supposed have led to this fatal catastrophe...'

MARY *is trying to reach out for* SHELLEY.

SHELLEY. Leave me alone!

MARY *recoils, freezes*. SHELLEY *exits*. CLAIRE *looks at* MARY, *appalled, and goes after him*.

Lights change. Back to widow MARY *again*.

CREATURE'S VOICE. Who made This? Who did This?

MARY. God help me, I am the author of her death!

Oh yes, this scandal never left us. Even when we were married and respectable. Respectable! With Harriet dead? The world blamed Shelley. Blamed us both.

Nothing for it, we were hounded back to Italy.

Pursued, we moved on. Shelley, me, our little William, our new little baby Clara, Claire and her little Allegra, with dark curls like her daddy's. One year, two years. My book was finished and forgotten, published in England. We moved on. Lucca, Livorno, marble piazzas, broken columns, sunshine, sewers... and no place we could call our home.

It was not my idea to send Claire's little Allegra to her father. Claire wanted to! She knew it was for the best, the best thing for the child...

Lights change. Back to somewhere in Italy, another new villa, around 1819.

Initial focus is on SHELLEY *with* CLAIRE, *whispering together.* MARY *elsewhere* (*near the desk*), *unpacking a box or crate, but she's hearing – and ignoring – them.*

SHELLEY. I will tell her. I'll tell her today. Hush!

CLAIRE. You promised!

She exits.

SHELLEY *goes to* MARY. *She looks up then continues her task.*

SHELLEY. Don't sulk, it isn't like you.

MARY. I'm not sulking, I'm unpacking. For about the twentieth time in five years.

SHELLEY. Not like my best, Mary…

MARY. You encourage her!

SHELLEY. Mary…

MARY. You do! It's pitiful. You heard her: 'Surely Byron will love me again' – it's degrading! After all this time? I'm afraid for her, she has less and less contact with reality.

SHELLEY. Reality? And what's so wonderful about reality?

MARY. It's not healthy!

Shelley, it tugs at my heart to see Claire grieve for her little girl… but, Shelley, who else was ever going to want Claire?

SHELLEY. Oh! – 'With Byron's little bastard brat hanging like a millstone round her neck?'

MARY. That is what the world is like, Shelley!

SHELLEY. A child is born with its own legacy of love. For fathers and mothers it can justly look to the whole human race.

MARY. In an ideal world, Shelley. Do you want Claire to live alone? For the rest of her life, with no one to love her?

SHELLEY. She has us.

Enter CLAIRE *with a packet.*

CLAIRE. A letter from Albé, look! I have a letter from him at last!

She tears it open, shakes out a single curl.

Empty. Empty. Empty except for a single dark curl. The lock of hair I begged him of Allegra's. But there's not a single word of her! Why doesn't he tell me she is well? My baby, I shouldn't have let her go!

MARY. Shelley had a letter too.

CLAIRE. Show it to me! Let me see it!

SHELLEY. Allegra is fine, Claire. Everything is well.

CLAIRE. What does he say about me?

SHELLEY. Nothing, Claire…

MARY. He says: 'Don't bring that damnable bitch, Madame Claire, near me. I promise to quit within the hour any town that have her in it.'

SHELLEY. Mary!

MARY. You have to be cruel to be kind, Shelley.

SHELLEY. Wrong, Mary! You have to be kind to be kind.

CLAIRE. Byron will love me again, when he sees how merry I am, and how slender I am, and how like that first summer, and how little Allegra needs her mother! Shelley says he'll take me to him. Didn't you, Shelley? You promised.

MARY. Did you? Did you promise to take her and leave me here?

MARY doesn't believe it. Then the dawning horror.
SHELLEY is squirming. SHELLEY's eyes signal to
CLAIRE to leave. She goes.

SHELLEY. Just till she sets her mind at rest Allegra is safe and well. You can come too, Mary. I'm sure we can find a villa near where Byron has the child. You know you don't like it here. Bagni di Lucca is so damp and gloomy, the whole town's a dull little fever-trap this season. Once you've had time to pack and settle everything, you should follow after with the children…

He puts his arm around MARY. *She flinches.*

MARY. Leave me!

SHELLEY *takes his arm away.*

SHELLEY. You can follow, soon. With the children.

Exit SHELLEY.

Lights change. Back to widow MARY *again.*

MARY. Oh, Shelley! How could you leave us like that?

Teething. I was convinced she was only teething.

Poor little Clara.

William was suffering from the heat too. I thought: 'Go to Shelley, go to Shelley and to Claire…'

When I got to the ferry at Fusina, she seemed much worse. I summoned a doctor. Poor little innocent, she seemed to recover. There was a mix-up with the passports, they tried to delay us. Press on, to Shelley and Claire. I honestly thought the best thing to do was to press on. Once I reached there… I thought… She was only teething, there was no reason to suppose… there seemed no good reason not to travel.

Oh, Clara, oh, my baby girl…

MARY *weeps, the shadows stir, someone's there.*

CREATURE'S VOICE. This killed the child. His name was *William.*

The name echoes.

MARY. William!

My dearest little Willmouse! How could you die and leave me still alive? When my Clara died, I thought it was the worst pain I ever had to bear. They said to me: 'You still have William, love your little boy.' Oh, William…

While I still grieved for my baby girl, I had to watch you sicken, some fever, no one knew the cause of it. I had to watch you burn and freeze and die in my arms, only nine months after Clara! Once I was a mother. Now I was a mother no more.

Lights change. Italy, another villa, the nursery. MARY *is packing a box again.* CLAIRE *comes.*

CLAIRE. What are you doing, Mary?

MARY. I am packing up William's clothes and toys. The nuns at the convent orphanage can perhaps make some use –

CLAIRE. Oh, Mary, my dear…!

ELISE *comes.*

Elise –

ELISE. Madame, let me help you.

MARY (*coldly*). I meant exactly what I said.

ELISE (*surprised*). Yes, madame.

MARY. You have until tomorrow morning to pack up your belongings.

ELISE (*sharply*). It won't take me that long, madame.

But then ELISE *sees what* MARY *is doing, is moved to pity.*

Oh, Mrs Shelley, it's not good for you to do such a sad task alone, let me help you, please.

MARY. I don't need your help, Elise.

ELISE. I'm grieving for him too! I've been with you since he was six months old. I loved your little Willmouse. I loved Baby Clara, and I loved Willmouse. Mr Shelley, he weeps in one room and you here all alone in another. It's not good for you to be alone with such dark thoughts. You should go to him.

MARY. By tomorrow morning, please. Go.

ELISE *exits*.

CLAIRE. Oh, Mary, is it true then?

MARY. Yes.

CLAIRE. It's Paolo's, I suppose?

MARY. So it would appear. Why?

CLAIRE. A maidservant lies down in the dark with a coachman with a twinkle in his eye. I don't know I can find it in my heart to blame her. Would you condemn your sister to banishment and poverty, and all for conceiving a child out of wedlock? It's only nature, Mary.

MARY. It's for her own good, Claire. They must marry at once, and we must leave this place; it has too many unhappy memories. Now that the summer is coming we need… Florence perhaps, or Genoa. But Elise must stay here and marry her coachman, we can't afford any more gossip.

CLAIRE. Put yourself in her place, Mary.

ELISE *marches back on*.

MARY. I didn't call you, Elise.

ELISE. No, madame, I came to take my leave. I think you are a cruel and heartless woman!

MARY. How dare you?

ELISE. Easily. Now that to tell the truth costs me nothing.

MARY. Elise!

ELISE. Yes, madame. And irresponsible, and a hypocrite too!

MARY. That's enough! Go, both of you, Paolo is waiting. You'll thank me some day.

ELISE. Thank you? For what?

MARY. A child needs a father. How can you, a servant of no fortune, manage to support a child?

ELISE. So free love is not to be afforded to the working classes?

MARY. Love is never free to any woman, Elise!

ELISE. How can you be her daughter and say that?

MARY. Because I am her daughter I must say that.

ELISE. Well, I read the book too! You were always encouraging me to improve my mind, even though I was only a maidservant! Indeed, I understand it very well; *The Rights of Woman*! The marvellous Mary Wollstonecraft was very keen on freedom for woman with six hundred a year, and a mill-owning husband to support her, and a bevy of maidservants sweeping and starching and giving suck to her squalling infants, not to speak of her rutting husband!

MARY *slaps her hard*.

Don't you think we are sisters? Are we not somewhat alike?

Enter SHELLEY.

SHELLEY. Mary, Elise, what's happening?

MARY. Go with Paolo! He is your husband. He is responsible.

ELISE *looks straight at* SHELLEY.

ELISE. Oh yes! *He* is responsible. (*She laughs.*)

ELISE *exits*.

SHELLEY. Mary, Mary…

MARY. He must marry her. She said so herself, he is the father!

SHELLEY. Of course he is, only…

MARY. Only what?

SHELLEY. The father! Father right and paternity have been used to enslave woman since time began.

MARY. Oh, Shelley…

SHELLEY. Elise is a brave girl.

CLAIRE. And a strong one.

MARY. – And I want her to survive.

SHELLEY. But to condemn any creature to a loveless marriage! All our recent suffering mustn't be allowed to make us hard.

MARY. Hard? It has turned my heart to ice!

Lights change. Widow MARY.

Oh yes. None may know the icy region this poor heart has encircled.

Once I was a mother. Now I was a mother no more.

Percy Florence, you will never know how much you mean to me.

CREATURE'S VOICE. Frankenstein, this must love!

MARY. Today the news came.

The worst.

I think before I tore open the letter, I knew it. Anxiety. Prognostications of evil. All week I've felt it approaching. Now here it is, this is what it was.

Lord Byron is dead.

Is it possible? The only one who had the courage to bring me the news I needed from that hellish day.

BYRON *appears, ghostly.*

BYRON. Yes, we burned him. The sublime Shelley. On the beach where he was washed up. Poured quicklime on and whoosh! Trelawney snatched his heart from the funeral pyre where it was not consumed, and put it in this leather pouch for you, Mrs Shelley.

MARY. Had it always, his heart…

BYRON. I loved him. We burned him. Then I couldn't wait to tear off my clothes and swim for miles and miles like a mad thing, wash the stench of burning flesh from off my skin and out of my hair. Couldn't wait to plunge myself in the Contessa.

BYRON *disappears*.

MARY. And now you're dead.

Dead at Missolonghi, Byron, gone to fight – why? – in someone else's war. Dead fighting for Greek independence.

I think of my last dead, my dear drowned Shelley, my own.

I think of my first dead, my mother I never knew.

I think of my little firstborn, in Poland Street, Shelley's lodgings, when I was scarce more than a child myself.

I think of Italy, Baby Clara, our own beloved Willmouse… There seemed no good reason not to travel…

They died, all my babies, and left Shelley and me all alone again.

Except for Claire.

Lights change. Italy. CLAIRE *is hectic, manic, rather than truly happy.*

CLAIRE. Didn't Shelley tell you?

MARY. Tell me?

CLAIRE. I'm going away, Mary. To Russia!

MARY. Russia! But, Claire, that's…

CLAIRE. Can't you see me? Queen of a Moscow schoolroom, mother hen to a brood of little princes and princesses? Isn't it so? Every other person in Russia seems to be royal nobility. It's Princess Irina this and Prince Misha, Prince Kolya that…

MARY. But it's so far away!

CLAIRE. Exactly. So the cold wind can sweep off the Steppes and blow the last tatters of my scarlet past away. Where, in all of Italy – or all of Europe – can I find one family that's not afraid to have the infamous Claire Clairmont teach its daughters?

MARY. Oh, Claire, you don't have to leave us.

CLAIRE. I must. No, Mary, I've been your millstone sister long enough.

MARY. And Allegra?

CLAIRE. She's with her father. And his whore Contessa! She's safe, she's well, and she has every luxury money can buy. It is time. I will go to Russia.

MARY. Oh, Claire! (*Hugs her.*)

CLAIRE. My best Mary too! Oh, Mary, how can you forgive me?

MARY. Ssh... Don't –

CLAIRE. But all the things I've said, when we've quarrelled! Too much love.

MARY. Too much alike, perhaps.

CLAIRE. I could cut my tongue out afterwards. Too passionate for my own good, your papa always said so...

Oh, Mary, when I said you were glad when Harriet died and you could be the respectable Mrs Shelley, I didn't mean it, you know that.

MARY. When do you leave?

CLAIRE. On the first of next month.

MARY. Go to Shelley, sing to him.

CLAIRE. Mary, promise me you won't sit here and get gloomy amongst all these shadows!

Lights change. Back to widow MARY.

MARY. Lies! Lies and malice!

That maid Elise made up a lot of silly stories and blabbed
them to some incredulous English expatriates we had been
friendly with once. Of course, they were only too happy to
believe them and tell the world!

But Byron should have defended us!

When the gossips talked, he should have told them it was not
true. Oh, Byron, you should have been our friend.

Lights change. Back in Italy. BYRON *comes.*

BYRON. Where is Shiloh? Where is my old friend, the Snake?

MARY. Not here. He won't speak to you, Byron, and you know
very well why!

BYRON. Do I?

MARY. Why, when we have never showed you anything but
kindness and affection, how can you return this by –

BYRON. Telling the truth? Allowing the truth to be told? Mary
Shelley, such hypocrisy from you, I should never have
expected it.

Well, Mrs Shelley, I can guess why you've sent for me. You
want to beg my daughter back. The answer is… no. The nuns
will bring her up good and God-fearing.

MARY. Byron, listen to me, I must…

BYRON. I asked myself, reasonably enough I should have
thought, whether Mademoiselle Claire Clairmont was the
right person to bring up Allegra. Does a mother know best?
Not, I suggest, if that mama is Claire. You see, fair Claire is
most keen that Allegra be at once our little secret, and at the
same time, bruited abroad as the dazzling daughter, albeit
wrong side of the blanket, of a Peer of the Realm.

An impossible desire, you might think; but then, Claire
Clairmont was never one to let impossibility stand in the way
of her desires.

MARY. Byron, I must tell you –

BYRON. Yes, Claire does take *mange*-ing her gateau and
having it to some ridiculous extremes.

MARY. You should have let us take Allegra, we would have
loved her like one of our own.

BYRON. Oh yes, like one of your own!

MARY. Another slander! I heard what you said, the Hoppners
told me!

'Have the Shelleys raised one? I do not want Allegra to die
of starvation and green fruit and to be brought up to believe
there is no Deity.'

You said that! How could you?

BYRON. So the gossipy Hoppners carried tittle-tattle! Well, I
cannot eat my words, would that I could swallow them
unsaid. And I should never have said them to your face,
Mary, I would not have looked in your eyes and wanted to
wound you.

I think you know how I grieved for you, little William too.

And your baby.

But think on it, Mary.

When our... mutual friends the Hoppners parroted out my
gaudy scrap of cruel wit, who or what exactly did they wish
to wound? My reputation in your eyes? Or did they wish to
wound you, Mary Shelley? Ask yourself.

MARY. Shelley does not love Claire.

BYRON. Love Claire? Of course Shelley does not love Claire,
even Claire has a hard job of it, loving Claire. I never pretended to love her, but if a girl of eighteen will come
prancing to a man at all hours, then there is but one way!

MARY. And did you defend us? When the Hoppners wrote you
that... unspeakable rumour, did you tell them it was all a lie?

BYRON. Unspeakable? Unspeakable? Don't be mim-mouthed, Mary, speak it out. If it is a lie, then look it in the face.

If you must know, Mrs Shelley, I told the Hoppners: 'Don't believe everything you hear from a dismissed servant – and if Elise says Claire Clairmont, not content with being the mother of Byron's brat, had to whelp herself on Shelley too, and was delivered of his sickly little scrap in the springtime, then I am sure it just a venomous lie, even though it would have been nine months or so from the time Shelley and Claire spent alone at my villa in Este...'

'Why, Mrs Hoppner,' I said, 'Shelley only accompanied Claire to prevail with me on her behalf.'

I said, 'Mrs Hoppner, can you believe that a man of Shelley's burning idealism could enter into a love affair with his wife's own sister – half sister, whatever – while his wife struggled alone across Europe with an ailing infant?' I said, 'There is not a word of truth in it, I swear on the head of my own Allegra.'

MARY. Well, she is dead! Your own Allegra!

BYRON *reels in shock and grief and gasps.*

The nuns wrote to us... to Claire, we've sent for her, to come home. No one could trace you, you were...

BYRON. Gadding about some spa with the Contessa. And my Allegra is dead. (*He sobs.*)

MARY. I tried to tell you, but you wouldn't listen. There has been an epidemic, it swept through the convent. Your little love child was among the first –

She goes to reach out. He shakes her off with hatred.

BYRON. No!

MARY. There is something wrong in how we all live.

BYRON. Oh yes, look in the mirror of my grief and see your-self. All men hate the wretched. That's one of yours, eh,

Mary? And the wretched hate each other. We are malicious because we are miserable.

Pleasure, freedom, wine, women, song, apes, peacocks, vinegar purges, boys, opium, ocean-going, orgies – I won't give up any of it, I'll double my gluttony and double it again.

All just to kill time, eh, Mary? It will be the death of me.

MARY. But we do not live as you do.

BYRON. Oh, I forgot. The Shelleys are political! The Shelleys are principled. The Shelleys do not eat dead animals. How about dead children?

MARY. Truly you are a monster!

The worst pain a mother ever bore, to have her children die before her!

BYRON. I will live with my guilt, can you live with yours?

MARY. I loved my children! And I will never cease from grieving, even when my new child is born!

BYRON. A new baby? Congratulations! And to Shiloh too, is there to be no end to this creation? Well, better luck this time, Mary!

MARY. I lived for my children.

BYRON. Well, I have never pretended to live for anyone but myself, and there's where we differ.

Infants do benefit from travel, don't they? Florence, Venice, Padua, a bit of culture and cholera does broaden the mind.

MARY. You are a twisted person!

BYRON. Oh yes, Mary, there is something in us which is very ugly. Do you not think we are somewhat alike? We are put together all wrong.

MARY. A monster!

BYRON. Well, if I am your monster, who, or what are you, Mary Shelley?

Yes, I have read your book. Very powerful it is, too.
Remarkable for a girl of… what were you? Nineteen? I'm
sure I can't imagine where you got your ideas from, can
you?

MARY. Damn that book! It's only a book, an idea!

BYRON. Have you read your book? Oh, I know you wrote it,
have you read it, though, recently? I'm sure it's silly of me to
read between the lines, though. No profit in noticing an
author name a character William after her beloved Baba,
blond curls and all, and then strangle him to death on page
sixty-nine! Oh, not many mamas, especially not busy-fin-
gered distracted mamas, who have not occasionally, *en
passant*, wished to silence the little darling!

MARY. I'm afraid of you!

BYRON. Don't be afraid, Mary. Courage! Where's Shiloh? He
wanted to see me.

Excuse me, Mrs Shelley, I'm just off to see a man about a
boat!

Exit BYRON.

Lights change. Back to widow MARY.

MARY. Oh, Byron; oh, Shelley –

And, in a flash, back to Italy again.

SHELLEY *comes.*

SHELLEY. Mary, Mary darling.

MARY. I wanted to die.

SHELLEY. Doctor says wait a while, and then we'll have
another.

MARY. Never! Never another!

SHELLEY. Come on. You're better, you are. No more blood.
Up, for a little while. I'll wrap you up, and our precious little
boy, and we'll walk, yes we will. Perciflo loves the seashore.

Come, Mary, a gentle walk with your husband and your little son in the clean air by the ocean.

MARY. Shelley, leave me here alone!

SHELLEY. Come and see her.

MARY. Your new love?

SHELLEY. Come and see her...

MARY. No.

SHELLEY. New arrived from Genoa, the bonniest boat that ever sailed the seas!

MARY. *The Don Juan.*

SHELLEY. *The Ariel*! Every sail unfurled! That other name won't stick, depend on it. She's *The Ariel*. It's not to be called in Byron's honour.

MARY. Yet it sailed in, monstrous letters blazoned across the mainsail, '*The Don Juan*'!

SHELLEY. You don't seem to care how much it grieves me that you won't sail with me.

MARY. I cannot! Shelley, I won't come because I cannot! I nearly died, Shelley.

SHELLEY. Oh, Mary, it was too soon. Too soon to have another, you hadn't your strength back after little Percy.

MARY. I nearly died. I didn't care if I died. I felt... I go to no new creation, I enter under no new laws. I thought all my life-blood is drained away. No pain. I'm going to die.

SHELLEY. I saved you!

MARY. I... am... in... pain. Inside it. It is a ship, and it's bearing me away.

SHELLEY. It was pure instinct, the ice.

MARY. My element. I swim in it and I do not die.

SHELLEY. You were losing so much blood, I had never seen so
much blood. I ran all the way to the Ice House. I woke
Umberto, made him pack the last shard of ice into the bath.
He said the shock would kill you, but I lifted you up in my
arms, and I plunged you into that bath of ice, and that
stopped the flow.

MARY. No baby. I have lost my last. Seven years, Shelley. I've
put three tiny coffins in the earth, lost two unborn babies in
the womb. Our union trails a cortège of dead infants in its
wake. Who cursed us? Were we cursed by our own
impossible dreams?

Never again, Shelley. Another way of making life, that's
what we need.

Another way to live…

SHELLEY. We have our sweet Perciflo, he's flourishing, and
when you've regained your strength, we can try again.

MARY. Never! I will never begin me another!

SHELLEY. I don't know how to make you happy!

MARY. I need a faithful mate, to be the true husband of my heart.

SHELLEY. And you have me!

MARY. Yes, I have you.

SHELLEY. That love we found, back in St Pancras
Graveyard…

MARY. By my mother's grave.

SHELLEY. Yes, she died. It's a terrible thing that her child bed
was her deathbed, Mary, but you didn't die.

But, oh yes! You're right, Mary. Yes, I am a man. I shall
never die in childbirth. Oh no, we're a different species.
Let's not try to communicate. The cracks appear. We are
each on smaller and smaller islands of ice, floating away
from each other, further and further away. Goodbye, Mary.

MARY. I don't want to be alone like this.

SHELLEY. Then reach out! Mary, I'll never turn from you. To
turn sometimes to others isn't to turn from you.

MARY. Oh, Shelley, to live in the spirit as much as you do puts
a great deal of strain on the body.

SHELLEY. Mary, darling, you're shivering. Come…

SHELLEY *tries to kiss her,* MARY *shrugs him off.*

MARY. Don't always try to kiss me when I try to talk to you!

SHELLEY. Mary, don't always talk at me when I try to kiss you.

MARY. Leave me alone, Shelley!

SHELLEY. Oh, Mary, I cannot reach you.

MARY. Sometimes, I think there's not a woman in the world
that hasn't fallen in love with you, and that you haven't
loved back! Oh yes, Shelley, I know 'True love differs from
gold and clay. To divide is not to take away…' I'm not
sixteen years old any longer! I've learned to suspect any
sentiment which rhymes that easily.

SHELLEY. Back in that graveyard, you said yes! You'd sail
away with me for ever. Don't turn back.

MARY. So I must make myself into the girl you saw in the
graveyard?

SHELLEY. The girl I know you to be!

Exit SHELLEY. *Lights change. Back to widow* MARY.

MARY. But I could not. I disappointed him. Have I a cold
heart? He turned to Jane Williams, she and Edward came
over from England to join us, share the villa, share –

She was my friend, we were widowed together, we waited
together all that last long week as we waited for news.

But all I really remember of that last summer as everything
fell to pieces all around us, was the boat, Ned Williams

singing sea shanties and Shelley, his head in pretty Jane
Williams's lap, and she playing the guitar and Shelley
making pretty songs for her!

Lights change. SHELLEY *comes again. Near the very end of
his life. Disintegration. In a trembling state.*

SHELLEY. Such a dream… God help me, Mary, but I cannot
shake it. You were in it. I was in it with you. You… got up
from your sickbed and walked naked towards me, your skin
all torn and tattered and bloodstained. You said, very brisk,
matter of fact – 'Get up, Shelley, the sea is invading the
house and it's all coming down!' I looked out on the terrace.
I thought I had wakened. I dreamed I was awake and the
boiling seas came pouring in. Then it changed. I saw my own
self, bending over you where you were stretched out
sleeping, and I was strangling you. Yesterday, I saw my own
ghost walking in the garden and it called out to me –

There is movement in the shadows and a cry.

CREATURE'S VOICE. How long do you mean to be content?

Lights change. Back to widow MARY.

MARY. Not long…

They only knew him by… in his pocket they found the
volume of Keats he'd been reading, bent open at the place
he'd reached in it. His face, his hands, all parts of him
not… protected by his clothing had been eaten away by the
fishes.

I wonder what it's like to drown? Did he expect to breath
easy in a brand-new element, plunge straight in, embracing
it? I wouldn't put it past him. What bobbed up at him from
the lone and level sands of the sea bottom?

Nymphs? Nereids? Mermaids? All the flimsy, impossible
women, glittering hermaphrodites, did they tangle with him,
did he clasp his sweet ideal at last? Or was he beating useless
limbs, dragged down by sodden duds among the

bladderwrack and nosing dogfish, fighting his way back, gulping and struggling with bursting lungs, back to his flesh and blood, Mary?

She gets together paper, quill.

I must write to Claire, tell her Lord Byron, her Albé, is dead.

Calmly, she begins to write.

Light fades.

The End.